Cornerstones of Freedom

The Story of

THE SAN FRANCISCO EARTHQUAKE

By R. Conrad Stein

Illustrated by Nathan Greene

 CHILDRENS PRESS, CHICAGO

Library of Congress Cataloging in Publication Data

Stein, R. Conrad.
 The story of the San Francisco earthquake.

 (Cornerstones of freedom)
 Summary: Describes the devastating earthquake and
ensuing fire that destroyed much of San Francisco in
the spring of 1906.
  1. San Francisco (Calif.)—Earthquake, 1906—
Juvenile literature. 2. San Francisco (Calif.)—Fire,
1906—Juvenile literature. [1. San Francisco (Calif.)—
Earthquake, 1906. 2. San Francisco (Calif.)—Fire,
1906] I. Greene, Nathan, 1961-   , ill. II. Title.
III. Series.
F869.S357S84 1983   979.4'61'051   83-10135
ISBN 0-516-04664-0   AACR2

San Francisco, California. April 18, 1906. 5:00 A.M.

The day promised to be marvelous. A rising sun painted long fingers of red and orange over the tall buildings downtown. Along the waterfront, waves lapped lazily against the docks.

But on this perfect spring morning something troubled the animals. Dogs howled in nearly every backyard. Horses neighed and pranced about nervously. A policeman named Jesse Cook noticed the strange behavior. Never before had he heard so many dogs locked in such long, eerie howls.

It was not known then that animals have a special early warning system to tell them of the coming of an earthquake. The pre-quake tensions that rumble deep below the ground send waves to the surface that can be heard only by animals. It is as though the earth is singing a special song meant only for special ears.

North of San Francisco and 150 miles out to sea, the schooner *John A. Campbell* steered toward the city. The water was calm. The crew looked forward to shore leave in their favorite port. Suddenly, the three-thousand-ton vessel jumped two feet out of the ocean. It seemed as if the hand of an invisible giant had seized the ship, held it above the water for a second, and then dropped it to splash back into the sea. No one was hurt. The puzzled crew looked up to the captain. The captain shrugged his shoulders. He had been a seaman for years, but never had he experienced such a sudden and mysterious lurch.

The ship had passed over the *focus* of the San Francisco Earthquake. The focus is the point where an earthquake begins. Masses of rock deep below the ocean floor were under unbelievable tension. Finally the rocks cracked, releasing a burst of energy that caused the ship to jump. The crack in the earth could be compared to the cut a seamstress makes in a piece of cloth. After the first cut, the cloth tears easily.

Some twenty-five miles beneath the ocean floor, the sudden rip in the earth arrowed toward shore. Like a demon freight train, the rip moved at the speed of seven thousand miles an hour. The grinding and shifting of billions of tons of rock generated more energy than all the explosives blown up in World War II.

The rip snaked to the right when it met the coastline two hundred miles north of San Francisco. In seconds, it altered landscapes that had stood unchanged for thousands of years. Masses of rock rose. Masses of rock fell. Yawning cracks opened in the earth. Stubby cliffs jutted up where there had once been flat land.

Down the lonely coastline the great tear in the earth spread. At times it swerved out to sea, but always it returned to gash the land like a giant plowshare. In the redwood forests, five-hundred-year-old trees were uprooted and tumbled down like matchsticks. In the coastal fishing villages, houses shuddered and fell in heaps.

Relentlessly, the rip swept south toward the sleeping city of San Francisco.

People who have survived a major earthquake claim they will always remember the sound. "It's deep, unbelievably deep. It will rattle your bones," they say. On a fine spring morning, the earthquake struck San Francisco with a roar that sounded like the devil's own drumroll.

Jesse Cook, the policeman walking his beat, was suddenly frozen in his tracks. "There was a deep rumble, deep and terrible," he said. "And then I could see it actually coming up Washington Street. The whole street was undulating. It was as if the waves of the ocean were coming toward me. . . . "

The skyline of San Francisco seemed to sway. Bells from a dozen different churches pealed as their steeples wobbled crazily. Hundreds of brick chimneys toppled over. People on the sidewalks were knocked flat, as if they had been hit by a truck. One man claimed that the ground under his feet shook "like a rat in the mouth of a terrier."

The earthquake caught most people sound asleep.
A visiting Englishman named Walter Bennett was
in bed in his hotel room when suddenly, "Every-
where there was the noise, like thousands of violins,
all at discord. The most harrowing sound one could
imagine." The Englishman bolted out of bed and
tried to reach his hotel window. The floor seesawed
beneath him. Plaster rained from the ceiling. He
stood, unable to move, hoping none of this was true.
Perhaps he was still asleep, in the grip of a terrible
nightmare.

Newspaper reporter James Hopper also was asleep in a hotel when the first shock, or tremor, struck. Hopper later wrote, "I awoke to the city's destruction. Right away it was incredible, the violence of the quake.... It pounced upon the earth like a bulldog." The reporter managed to look out his window. "I heard the roar of bricks coming down and twisted girders. Then the rear of my building for three stories upward fell. The mass struck a series of little wooden houses in the alley below. I saw the bricks passing through the roofs as though they were tissue paper. I had this feeling of finality. This is death."

Just as suddenly as it began, the quake stopped.

Now the people heard a new noise. To some it sounded like the squeal of a thousand nails being pulled out of wooden beams. The new noise was the wailing of buildings slowly toppling over.

Then a second tremor struck.

Again, the houses and buildings seemed to dance together in a slow waltz. Bricks, plaster, and jagged pieces of window glass showered the streets. Once more, the incredibly deep roar rumbled up from the belly of the earth.

Finally, the second tremor ended. A strange, frightening hush fell on the city. Reporter Hopper found the sudden stillness to be almost as terrifying as the roar of the quake. "Throughout the big quaking I had not heard a cry, not a sound, not a sob, not a whisper. And now when the roar was over, and only a brick fell here and there, this silence was an awful thing. Then, in the alley below, someone began to groan. It was a woman's groan, soft and low."

All over the city, thousands of other injured and shocked people were groaning.

Two sharp tremors rattled San Francisco that morning. The first struck at 5:12 A.M. and lasted about forty seconds. Then came a ten-second gap. It was followed by another violent tremor about fifteen seconds in length. The entire earthquake, including the ten-second interval, lasted between sixty-five and seventy-five seconds. To the people of the city it seemed like an eternity.

Whole neighborhoods were suddenly rearranged. Wooden row houses that once had stood neatly in a line were now twisted about. Many were leaning on each other. In the houses, people parted their curtains and were horrified to discover that the view they beheld from their bedroom windows was entirely different from the one they had been looking at for years.

The downtown section was a shambles. Streets were buried under piles of bricks and plaster. Cable-car tracks lay twisted like impossibly long snakes. Broken high-voltage wires danced on the sidewalks and sent out showers of orange sparks. Brick walls of many new buildings had collapsed, leaving their steel frames standing like monstrous birdcages.

On the rubble-filled streets came the cries of people. Desperate screams were heard from men and women still alive but buried under tons of debris. Panicky mothers shouted for their children. Husbands called for their wives.

From the Palace Hotel came the strangest sound

of all. Three stories up, the world-famous opera singer, Enrico Caruso, stood singing through a shattered window. The night before, Caruso had thrilled San Francisco operagoers with his performance in *Carmen*. This morning, the singer was terrified that the quake had somehow frightened away his voice. To test his golden voice, Caruso burst into song. Satisfied that his voice retained all its old ringing power, he continued to sing. So the words of grand opera mingled crazily with the cries of the injured and dying people.

A different and more chilling sound worried San Franciscans. From below the sidewalks came the gurgling of water and the hissing of escaping gas. Underground lay a spider's web of pipes. The quake had twisted and snapped those pipes as if they were pretzels. Water gushed out of water pipes. Gas flowed from gas lines. Any spark could ignite the gas, and the firemen would have no water pressure to fight the fires.

More than any other disaster, San Franciscans feared fire. Fires had devastated the city again and again during its brief but spectacular history.

Sixty years before the earthquake, San Francisco was just one of several settlements the Spaniards had established on the California coast. For decades the city was called Yerba Buena—Spanish for mint, or "good herb." The United States took California from Mexico in 1846. The next year Yerba Buena's name was changed to San Francisco. At the time, the tiny port city held about eight hundred people. Then, in 1848, a ranch foreman stumbled upon gold about one hundred miles inland.

Gold! The word rifled across the United States and swept the world. People hoping to become overnight millionaires scrambled to California. Most began their search for riches in the port of San Francisco.

By 1850, the city's population had zoomed to 35,000. And shiploads of newcomers arrived each day. To accommodate this flow, wooden stores and houses were hammered together in a matter of weeks. Whole neighborhoods with streets, churches, and schools spread out to cover land where cows had grazed just a year earlier.

Even after the Gold Rush, Californians discovered a new way to earn fortunes. In 1869, a golden spike marked the completion of the first transcontinental railroad. The port of San Francisco was now connected by rail to the sprawling markets in the East. Railroad prosperity kept the city rich and growing. By 1900, San Francisco's population stood at more than a third of a million, making it the ninth largest city in the United States.

However, the hastily constructed wooden buildings were easy prey for fires. A monstrous fire leveled the city on Christmas Eve, 1849. Just three years later, another runaway blaze left San Francisco in ashes. As the city spread over the many hills, hardly a year passed without a major fire breaking out in some neighborhood.

To battle their plague of fires, San Franciscans developed the best fire department in the West. Firemen became heroes. They marched in parades and were showered with confetti and flowers. Even today, two San Francisco monuments honor heroic fire fighters of the city's past. No other city in the world adored its firemen as did the people of old San Francisco.

But the quake of 1906 seemed to have an almost-human determination to destroy the city. During the first jarring seconds, the bedroom floor holding Fire Chief Dennis Sullivan caved in and the chief fell three floors to his death. The second tremor destroyed the city's Central Fire Alarm System. Finally, the heaving earth shattered the pipes leading to the fire hydrants. Without their leader, and especially without water, the best fire fighters in the West were helpless.

In the fifteen minutes following the quake, more than fifty separate fires were reported in the downtown section alone. Many had been set by sparks from broken electric lines. From other points in the city, columns of smoke swirled into the sky. Fire, the old scourge of San Francisco, had raised its head once more.

Afraid of the fires, people swarmed out of their houses and headed for the waterfront or to the parks. Then, as now, San Francisco was the home of men and women from many different lands. The streets became a babble of languages. Chinese families pushed through the crowds carrying huge sacks on their backs. Italians loaded their possessions on pushcarts. Well-to-do second- and third-generation Americans tried to escape the fire in their horse-drawn buggies. Even one or two primitive motorcars joined the procession.

In Chinatown, a great commotion broke out. An enormous black bull that had escaped from a pen was rumbling down the crowded streets. Blood flowed from wounds on the animal's flanks and saliva oozed from its mouth. People on the streets scurried away from the raging beast. But as soon as the bull stopped to catch its breath, the people pelted it with stones and shouted at it. An ancient Chinese legend says the world is supported on the backs of four enormous bulls. Many Chinatown residents believed this runaway bull had caused the earthquake. "Go home to your brothers!" they shouted. "The world needs you to hold it up." Finally, the wounded bull galloped out of Chinatown and into a square where a policeman shot it dead.

As choking clouds of black smoke grew thicker, a fresh disaster struck the city. West of downtown, a woman surveyed the damage the quake had done to her home. Her windows were broken and clumps of plaster had fallen off the ceiling. Still, her home was in fairly good shape. And the big fires were miles away from her neighborhood. So the woman decided to cook breakfast for her family just as she would on any other morning. Unknown to her, the quake had damaged the inside of her chimney. When she lit her wood-burning stove, sparks set the roof on fire. Surrounding roofs were quickly set ablaze. Historians later called this the "ham and eggs" fire. It set ablaze a neighborhood where there were many older wooden houses.

During the afternoon, the wind picked up. It whooshed off the waterfront and whipped through the city. Dozens of small fires merged to become one devouring sheet of flame. In some sections, the great fire began moving as fast as a man can run.

While the fire raged, San Francisco Mayor Eugene Schmitz met with army commander General Frederick Funston. Since there was no water, the general wanted to fight the fire with dynamite. He planned to create a firebreak by blasting a row of

houses in the fire's path. But the mayor feared he would make powerful enemies if he blew up the homes of rich San Franciscans.

The general and the mayor argued while the fire grew as it swept each new block. At its peak, some people claimed the flames towered a mile high. A photographer named Moshe Cohen ran through the streets almost in the middle of the inferno. Miraculously he escaped, and left this description: "There was flame and noise and hell. The whole city seemed to be drowning in flame. The flames and smoke seemed to have a life of their own. Together they seemed alive, writhing all over the place with a sound that nobody had heard before. It wasn't a normal fire sound. No, this was a *chattering...* chattering like a billion monkeys were on the run."

As evening approached, nearly every citizen of San Francisco was heading out of the city, trying to stay a step ahead of the fire. "It was a single file of silent human beings," wrote a woman named Bertha Nienberg. "Their eyes were large and white against cinder-blackened faces.... Each carried something, a birdcage, a flowerpot, a vase, a puppy, a cat, a picture. There was no sign of tears. No moans, no shrieks, no hysteria. It was a dignified procession."

By dawn of the second day, Mayor Schmitz and General Funston finally agreed to blast a firebreak along Van Ness Avenue. It was the widest street in the city and separated old San Francisco from the newer suburbs to the west. Both dynamite and cannons were used in the blasting. The thundering explosions made it sound as if a war had broken out in the beleaguered city.

The general and the mayor also agreed to take stern steps against stealing. Signs were hastily printed up and nailed on standing walls:

PROCLAMATION BY THE MAYOR

The Federal troops have been authorized by me to KILL any and all persons found engaged in looting or in the commission of any other crime.

Several people who were caught looting were shot and killed by soldiers. The exact number of executions is unknown. But in the days following the disaster, General Funston's troops were harshly criticized by the people. They claimed that the general's men were trigger-happy. Witnesses reported that soldiers were shooting people who were sifting through the rubble of their own homes looking for their own valuables.

While there was some looting, most San Franciscans behaved in a very civilized manner. Men and women carried injured people through the streets as the fire roared at their backs. Often a person who had only one piece of bread divided it and gave half to a perfect stranger who had no bread at all.

The twin disasters of earthquake and fire turned some very ordinary people into heroes. Mailmen using mail sacks beat down the flames that threatened their post office. At St. Mary's, a priest risked his life to save his church. The priest climbed the nearly vertical roof of the church and batted away sparks with a cloth bag. Seeing the black-robed figure clinging to the roof lifted the spirits of the neighbors. "When he had won, he just hung there supporting himself with one hand," wrote one spectator. "For a moment, the crowd did nothing. Then someone shouted that we had just witnessed a miracle. Everybody was cheering like crazy. It was incredible."

A reporter named Henry Lafler told how the people of Russian Hill saved their own neighborhood. "It was the boys of the hill who saved the hill. It was Toby Irwin the prizefighter, and Tim O'Brien who works in the warehouse.... It was the old Irish woman who had hoarded a few buckets of water through the fear and rumors and who came painfully toiling up the slope with water for the fire. It was the poor peasant Italian with a barrel of cheap wine in his cellar who now rolled it out and broke its head with an ax, and with dipper and bucket fought the fire till he dropped. It was Sadie who works in the box factory and Annie who is a coat finisher and Rose who is a chocolate dipper in a candy shop. . . . It was they who saved the hill."

Toward the evening of the second day, the blaze had pushed up to the firebreak on Van Ness Avenue. Soldiers and firemen had worked feverishly, but the blasting was still incomplete. At several points, the fire skipped over the firebreak. Exhausted firemen fought back, using water from backyard pumps, artesian wells, and even rain barrels. At Van Ness Avenue, they finally halted the fire's westward advance.

The fight now shifted to the east, along the waterfront. San Francisco's most important link to the outside world was its shipping docks. If those docks burned down, rebuilding the city would be far more difficult. At the waterfront, navy fireboats streamed a thousand gallons of water a minute onto

the blaze. Fire trucks also pumped water out of the bay and hosed it onto the fire. For hours, the battle with the raging inferno dragged on.

Then suddenly the wind shifted. It blew the fire back over ground it had already covered. And soon it began to rain. By the morning of April 21, 1906, the great San Francisco fire was out. It had lasted a hellish seventy-four hours.

Dazed San Franciscans surveyed the ruins of their once-proud city. The fire had leveled three thousand acres of houses and buildings. About seven hundred people were dead. No one knows whether the earthquake or the fire was the bigger killer. A quarter of a million people were homeless. Property losses were estimated at five hundred million dollars.

Despite the enormity of the disaster, the people began rebuilding. Even while the bricks were still hot, workers cleared rubble from the streets. Families set up tents on the ashes of their old homes and started cleaning up the mess. Signs designed to amuse the neighbors soon popped up on the tents. Above one tent a sign read, "Ring bell for landlady." Another sign poked fun at San Francisco's neighbor city: "Cheer up! Tomorrow we might have to move to Oakland."

With astonishing speed, a new city rose from the debris of the old. Within three years, more than twenty thousand new buildings had been constructed. Most were made of brick and steel and were far superior to the ones they replaced. No longer would San Franciscans have to fear the old curse of runaway fire. Ten years after the earthquake, not a trace of damage could be found anywhere in the city.

Although San Franciscans built a gleaming new city, they could never forget the nightmare of 1906. The thought of a major new earthquake still haunts the people.

San Francisco lies in what scientists call "earthquake country." This is an area where earthquakes are likely to occur. Before the great quake, tremors had destroyed parts of the city in 1865 and again in 1868. In modern times, a severe quake rattled the San Francisco area in 1957.

Much of California sits on top of a geological formation called the San Andreas Fault. A fault is an ancient break in the earth. At a fault line, massive layers of rock tilt together almost like two eaves of a slanted roof. Many miles below the ground, the layers float on a sea of hot, liquified rock. When the layers shift suddenly along the fault line, an earthquake will occur. The violence of the earthquake will depend on the degree of shifting. A sudden horizontal snap of just twenty feet produced the great quake of 1906.

San Francisco is also dangerously close to another fault line—the Hayward Fault. Either one of these two faults could snap and create a new disaster. Many scientists believe the people of San Francisco are living on top of a ticking time bomb. One scientist at Berkeley, California, recently said that the next big earthquake "could come tonight or tomorrow—it will certainly come within the next fifty years." Other scientists differ. They say a century will pass before California feels another great quake. Nearly all scientists agree, however, that someday the San Andreas Fault will snap again. Then a terrible earthquake will rock the entire Pacific Coast.

Certainly the fear of an earthquake has not kept people from coming to San Francisco. The climate is gentle. The city is exciting and beautiful. Every year, thousands of newcomers flock to the city by the bay. They come hoping to find a new way of life. As they did more than a century ago, men and women look upon San Francisco as a city of endless promise.

About the Author

R. Conrad Stein was born and grew up in Chicago. He enlisted in the Marine Corps at the age of eighteen, and served for three years. He then attended the University of Illinois, where he received a Bachelor's Degree in history. He later studied in Mexico and earned a Master of Fine Arts degree from the University of Guanajuato.

The study of history is Mr. Stein's hobby. Since he finds it to be an exciting subject, he tries to bring the excitement of history to his readers. He is the author of many other books, articles, and short stories written for young people.

Mr. Stein is married to Deborah Kent, who is also a writer of books for young readers.

About the Artist

Nathan Greene is a recent graduate of the American Academy of Art in Chicago, where he studied Fine Art and Illustration. He lives in Berrien Springs, Michigan, and enjoys backpacking, running, and, of course, art. Mr. Greene is just beginning a freelance career in illustration. This is his first book.

Weekly Reader Books offers several exciting
card and activity programs. For information,
write to WEEKLY READER BOOKS, P.O. Box 16636,
Columbus, Ohio 43216.